W9-BKN-819

THIS IS NOT THE HONEYMOON I ANTICIPATED

Dick Hafer

KALMBACH BOOKS

© 1996 by Dick Hafer. All rights reserved. This book may not be reproduced in part or in whole without written permission of the publisher, except in the case of brief quotations used in reviews. Published by Kalmbach Publishing Co., 21027 Crossroads Circle, Waukesha, WI 53187. Telephone: (414) 796-8776.

Printed in the United States of America

Publisher's Cataloging in Publication
(Prepared by Quality Books Inc.)

Hafer, Richard.
    This is not the honeymoon I anticipated / Dick Hafer.
    p. cm.
    ISBN 0-89024-302-6

    1. Railroads—Models—Caricatures and cartoons.   2. American wit and humor, Pictorial.   I. Title.

NC1429.H285A4 1996   741.5'973
                              QBI96-40125

Dedication....

To all of you who have bought my books. This allowed me to get *much* more neat train stuff!

Now, if you'll just purchase lots of these books for your friends and relatives . . . well, there's this custom-built Reading T-1 loco that I've been slobbering over. . . .

Special thanks to Marlin Cohen, Tom Wertz, and Mary—my wife, editor, co-idea-generator, and best friend.

dick hafer

DO YOU PROMISE TO LOVE, HONOR . . .
AND LET HIM HAVE ALL THE TRAINS HE WANTS?

I DON'T CARE HOW CLEAN IT GETS YOUR TRACK. . . . PUT KITTY DOWN!!

DEAR ME . . . THESE OLD TRAINS CAN'T BE WORTH MUCH. EDWIN NEVER
BOTHERED TO TAKE THEM OUT OF THE BOX. . . . AND HE OFTEN SAID
THAT MOST OF THEM WERE NEVER PUT "INTO PRODUCTION," SO THEY
COULDN'T HAVE BEEN VERY POPULAR. IS $10 FOR EVERYTHING TOO MUCH?

BUT I CAN'T COME IN TO WORK TODAY, BOSS. . . .
THE MOTOR ON MY GP-38 DIED LAST NIGHT!

. . . AND FOR USING ROLLER BEARING TRUCKS ON A PRE-1955 BOXCAR KIT . . .

YEAH . . . I'M PLANNING ON FINALLY STARTING MY LAYOUT NEXT MONTH!

11

NO . . . YOU SEE, THE THEORY BEHIND "KITBASHING"
IS TO USE ROUGHLY SIMILAR KITS.

THIS IS THE REINFORCING MESH YOU'LL USE FOR MY WIFE'S HERNIA
OPERATION?!! WOW! IT'S PERFECT HO CHAIN LINK FENCE!! DOC . . . YOU
THINK MAYBE YOU COULD LET TWO OR THREE FEET HANG OUT
AND I COULD CUT IT OFF AS I NEED IT?!!

SHE'S SO BEAUTIFUL! I ONLY SAW HER IN THE BOX, WHEN HE BOUGHT US. IF ONLY THE BIG GUY WOULD MOVE ME OVER BY THE PLASTICVILLE DRUG STORE, WHERE SHE'S STANDING!

WE NEED MILK?!! GOOD GRIEF! YOU'D SEND ME OUT INTO THIS BLIZZARD FOR SOMETHING AS UNIMPORTANT AS MILK?!! WOW! YOU WANT ME TO DIE?!!

BUT I GOTTA GO OUT!! I'VE GOT TO DRIVE OVER TO BURRETT'S TRAINS TO PICK UP A PAIR OF COUPLERS! BE REASONABLE!!

YOUR LIVE STEAMER DOESN'T SEEM TO BE WORKING VERY WELL!

WHAT?!! MY GG1 HASN'T COME IN YET?!! I ORDERED IT FOUR YEARS AGO!!

I SAID, "PUT SOME **PIERS** UNDER THE TRESTLE"!!

DOUG . . . HAVE YOU EVER HEARD THE PHRASE "GET A LIFE"?

KEVIN WAS VERY PROUD OF HIS SCRATCHBUILT PICKLE CAR.

OH, GREAT! NOW WHERE DID THAT TINY COUPLER SPRING GET TO?!!

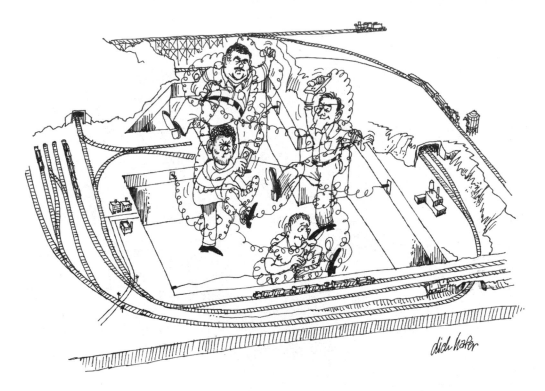

WALK-AROUND THROTTLE DRAWBACK #1

THERE'S GOT TO BE SOMETHING THAT SETS SLOWER THAN SUPER GLUE!

23

WENDELL!!

JOHN ARMSTRONG AS A CHILD

WHO SAID YOU CAN'T TAKE IT WITH YOU?

"HARPS"? OH, NO. YOU'VE BEEN ASSIGNED A 300 x 500-FOOT TRAIN ROOM!

29

THE ULTIMATE MODULAR RAILROAD

... AND ALL THE OTHER KIDS HAD MODEL TRAINS! BUT OH, NO ... I WAS TOO GROWN UP TO "PLAY WITH TRAINS"!!

ANDY, I AGREE WITH OUR WIVES. LET'S TAKE A NIGHT OFF FROM
RAILROADING AND WATCH VIDEOS WITH THEM.
LET'S SEE . . . HOW ABOUT "STRANGERS ON A TRAIN," OR "MURDER ON THE
ORIENT EXPRESS," OR "UNION PACIFIC," OR "3:10 TO YUMA," OR
"THE GREAT TRAIN ROBBERY," OR "RUNAWAY TRAINS," OR . . . ?

TURN OFF THAT POWER PACK AND GO TO SLEEP!!

HARRY!! YOU MENTIONED THAT YOU WERE GOING TO
BUILD A "HELIX." WHAT DOES A "HELIX" LOOK LIKE?!!

OPEN WIDE! HERE COMES THE TRAIN INTO THE TUNNEL!

CAN'T EVER REALLY LET IT GO, CAN YOU, CHESTER?

I DON'T CARE WHAT "MODEL RAILROADER" SAYS. . . .
I DON'T THINK THAT CORK ROADBED LOOKS REALISTIC!!

YEAH . . . IT WAS FREE! IT WAS JUST
STANDING THERE NEXT TO THE TRACKS!!

ONLY FOUR MORE HOURS 'TIL IT OPENS!!

... AND THIS IS OUR ACCURATE MODEL OF THE TEHACHAPI PASS. FOUR OF US WENT OUT WEST FOR 2½ MONTHS AND SIFTED DESERT SAND TO HO SCALE! IT JUST DOESN'T COME ANY MORE AUTHENTIC THAN THIS!

C'MON, BUDDY! CAN'T YOU WAIT JUST A LITTLE BIT?!!

NO. 4619

THE "BUNNYHOPPER." THREE PROTOTYPES PRODUCED.
INTRODUCED AT 1951 TOY FAIR. LOTS OF LAUGHS. ZERO SALES.
PRODUCTION CARS NEVER RELEASED, BUT DESIGNER WAS.

REJECTED TINPLATE DESIGNS

NO. 9263

THE "DEPRESSED-CENTER TRASH RECYCLING TRASH FLATCAR."

ONE PROTOTYPE PRODUCED IN 1953. DESIGNED BY ENVIRONMENTAL VISIONARY. HE WAS REASSIGNED TO ENVISION THE COMPANY TRASH INTO THE DUMPSTER.

PLANNED FOR USE WITH THE 17433 TRASH UNLOADER. NEITHER WERE EVER MASS-PRODUCED.

NO. 4276

"THUNDERSTORM CAR." ONE PROTOTYPE PRODUCED. THIS HIGHLY ANTICIPATED OPERATING CAR NEVER WENT INTO PRODUCTION, DUE TO AN UNFORTUNATE TEST ACCIDENT, IN WHICH THE ORIGINAL MODEL AND THE ENTIRE DESIGN TEAM WERE VAPORIZED.

JUST LET ME SET MY FOOD DOWN HERE, WHILE I LOOK AT YOUR STUFF!

IT'S SO NICE TO SEE A HUSBAND STAY HOME AND BE SO HAPPY WITH HIS HOBBY, INSTEAD OF BEING OUT EVERY NIGHT!

I'M NOT IMPRESSED. IT'S NOT BRASS!

O GAUGE?!! WHO'D EVER BUY IT?! IT'LL NEVER HOLD THE
TRACK PROPERLY. . . . AND HOW CAN KIDS' LITTLE HANDS
PUT THAT TINY STUFF ON THE TRACK?!

WELL, DON'T BLAME ME! I TOLD YOU TO PLAN IN SOME ACCESS HATCHES!

HOW LONG HAS IT BEEN SINCE YOU WORKED ON
YOUR GARDEN RAILROAD, DUANE?

JERRY . . . THIS ISN'T WHAT M.R. MEANT WHEN IT DISCUSSED
PHOTOMURAL BACKGROUNDS!

ACTUALLY, "STACK" CARS MEANS . . .

HOW COME YOU DON'T CARRY THE NORTH DAKOTA CENTRAL RAILROAD?
YOU DON'T CARRY ANYTHING!!

HERE'S MY CREDIT CARD!! THIS WILL TAKE AN 18-INCH RADIUS, WON'T IT?

THE DAY WILLARD DISCOVERED THE SOLUTION TO THE "CLOUD PROBLEM."

SPECTACULARLY POOR PLANNING AT THE MODULAR LAYOUT EXHIBIT

WELL, EVERY MUSEUM HAS TO START SOMEWHERE!

IT'S A NEW MODEL RAILROADING VIDEO THAT TEACHES
ME HOW TO MAKE MODEL RAILROADING VIDEOS!

WELL . . . MY GUESS IS THAT YOU'VE GOT A ROUGH
SPOT ON THE TRACK. . . . RIGHT ABOUT THERE.

BOY! TONIGHT'S GONNA BE A BIG ONE! FIRST THE ORE TRAIN IS GOING TO
THE STEEL MILL IN PITTSBURGH. WHILE IT'S UNLOADING, A FAST FREIGHT
WILL HEAD WEST TO YOUNGSTOWN AND A PASSENGER TRAIN, HEADED BY
AN A-B-A PA-1, WILL HIGHBALL IT INTO TOLEDO! MEANWHILE, WE'LL BE SPOT-
TING CARS ONTO THE VARIOUS INDUSTRIAL SIDINGS AND . . .

GOLLY! I THOUGHT A SCALE SNOWMAN WOULD MAKE YOU HAPPY, DAD!

YEAH, THIS LITTLE HOBBY SANDBLASTER DOES A FANTASTIC JOB!
IT REALLY . . . NOW, WHERE DID THAT ENGINE GET TO?

WOW! NOW THAT'S REALISTIC SMOKE!!

YOU MAY BE OVERDOING THE WEATHERING ON THAT REEFER JUST A BIT!

. . . AND A SIX-PACK OF WESTERN MARYLAND HOPPERS!

WOW! A COMMAND-CONTROL
SYSTEM THAT YOU DESIGNED
AND BUILT BY YOURSELF?!!

THE NEW CHICAGO COMMUTERS' MODULAR RAILROAD CLUB

IT'S AMAZING HOW MUCH OPERATION YOU CAN FIT INTO AN 8 X 9-FOOT ROOM!

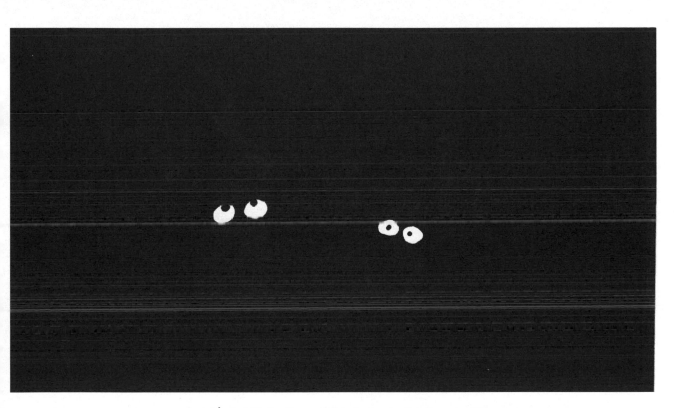

WOW! A REAL HO OPERATING COAL MINE!!

C'MON! . . . JUST FIVE MINUTES MORE . . . PLEASE?

SEE HOW THE WHEELS ON THIS SIDE ARE INSULATED!
THE REASON FOR THAT IS . . .

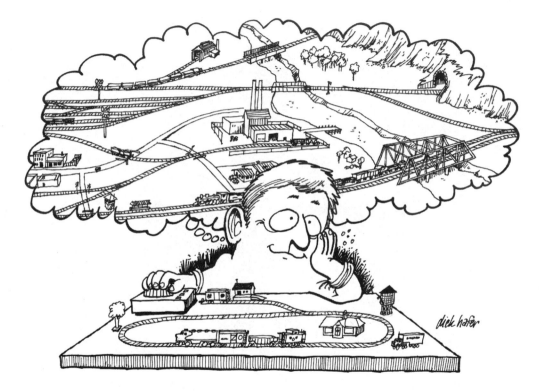

ARE YOU SURE THERE ISN'T SOME SPACE WE COULD FIND DOWNSTAIRS?

I UNDERSTAND THERE'S SUPPOSED TO BE A MODEL TRAIN SHOW
AROUND HERE SOMEWHERE. CAN YOU TELL ME WHERE IT'S AT?

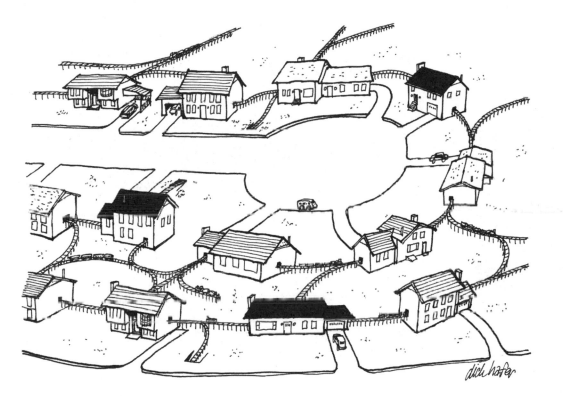

WHEN THE MODEL RAILROADING CRAZE HIT WESTERVILLE

JUST WATCH! I'VE BEEN STANDING HERE FOR SEVEN YEARS
AND THAT TROLLEY'S NEVER STOPPED ONCE FOR ME!!

WOW! GREAT WALLPAPER!!

WHY MUST I GROW UP?